MW01255081

BLOTTO

BOTANY

BLOTTO

A LESSON IN HEALING CORDIALS

AND PLANT MAGIC

Spencre L.R. McGowan

MORROW
GIFT

An Imprint of WILLIAM MORROW

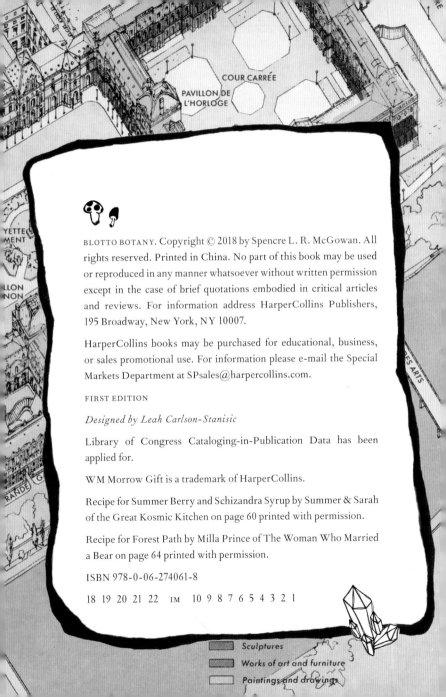

HarperCollins books may be purchased for educational, business, or sales promotional use. For information please e-mail the Special Markets Department at SPsales@harpercollins.com.

FIRST EDITION

Designed by Leah Carlson-Stanisic

Library of Congress Cataloging-in-Publication Data has been applied for.

WM Morrow Gift is a trademark of HarperCollins.

Recipe for Summer Berry and Schizandra Syrup by Summer & Sarah of the Great Kosmic Kitchen on page 60 printed with permission.

Recipe for Forest Path by Milla Prince of The Woman Who Married a Bear on page 64 printed with permission.

ISBN 978-0-06-274061-8

18 19 20 21 22   IM   10 9 8 7 6 5 4 3 2 1

To my mother and her mother . . .

And Emilia of Rosenhill, for putting me in the kitchen . . .

And my father, the chef.

Contents

Autumn 35

Winter 45

Shrubs   67

Bitters   73

Materia Medica   81

Self-Care   95

Introduction

I have loved plants for as long as I can remember. Growing up as the daughter of a chef, fresh herbs were commonplace on our dinner plates. I can recall chopping up wild chives from our yard in Massachusetts with a plastic knife and feeding them to my gracious circle of stuffed animals. My love for wild things grew from there, mainly through books and the broad imagination I developed growing up as an only child. The verdant woods and gardens I dreamed of were untamed and overgrown and my potion cupboards were always fully stocked.

I spent the summer after high school on a farm outside of Stockholm, collecting elderflower, baking with fresh rose petals, and grinding stinging nettles into flour, all the while unaware of the medicinal potency of each plant. It wasn't until the following summer back home on Nantucket that I happened upon the practice of using herbs as medicine with a friend who was also new to herbalism. From there, we spent many hours rummaging through fields and seaside brambles, our bicycle baskets filled to the brim with berries, weeds, and twigs. Our knees and palms were often scratched and dirtied from inspecting greens close to the ground, but the untold possibilities of these medicinal plants we collected always put our aches to rest.

A few years later, I attended the California School of Herbal Studies, where I truly delved into my practice as a medicinal herbalist, writer, and kitchen witch. Three days a week, I would wind my way down a narrow dirt road to a small red barn nestled into an emerald-covered valley. It was in that barn that I uncovered the deep history and value of cordials. Toward the end of the program, we were asked to create two different cordials and bring them along to a cordial party as one of our finals. This cordial party was considered a formal event. By which I mean as formal as you can get in a barn in the middle of the Redwoods with a bunch of plant-loving nerds, draped in lace and drunkenly jumping up and down to the nineties' top hits. It really was a magical night. Dozens of bottles lined the long center table, which bowed from years of use. The laughter and merriment that night cemented my already deep love of cordials and now here I am, sharing that love with you.

What I love about cordials is the real laid-back formulation process. They're quick to use up, which is perfect for someone who travels often. And in a pinch, they can infuse overnight, making perfect last-minute gifts (my specialty) or barbecue contributions. I almost always use something called the folk method in my herbal practice. Folk method is the practice of using a sense of intuition while making herbal remedies rather than the standard, ratio-to-ratio measurements found in many cookbooks today. Many of these recipes include measurements as guidelines, but listening to my own gut and the plants has always been a little more suited to my style, and I encourage you to do the same.

Blotto Botany started out as a self-published zine, something I made while living in a tiny farmhouse attic in Maine. It serves as a constant reminder to do what I love and listen to both my gut and plant allies. Here within the pages of this book, I invite you to make of these recipes what you will. Expand on them, love them, swap plants, swap spirits. This book is meant to be a look into an herbalist's log; a variety of experiments and delicious concoctions intended to sprout new ideas and connect you with tradition.

Drink to your health, your ancestors, and your friends. Make zines, write daily, make plant friends, and stay true to your own tastes and well-being.

What is a Cordial?

My first encounter with cordial making was not a pretty picture. I bought a fifth of cheap brandy and chopped up a knob of ginger, tossed both ingredients in a jar, and hoped for the best. Over the weeks that followed, I would periodically take the jar off its shelf and shake the contents within. Nothing seemed to be happening; no color transformation or real taste change had taken place, and I grew discouraged with the small ginger potion. This was before I went to herb school or had any real knowledge of what a cordial is and what it takes to make a good one. This was also before I understood the deep history and lore that is entwined with cordials.

Cordials have been used for generations to heal, soothe, and nourish. The earliest recorded writings of cordial usage date back to the thirteenth century, when they were most commonly used as medicine. It wasn't out of the ordinary for cordials to be made with gold, pearls, and coral, all believed to revive the body and spirit. Today, cordials are made to be enjoyed both as medicine and for pleasure (and with much more agreeable ingredients).

When it comes to drinks, there are multiple definitions of the word *cordial*. In Europe, cordials are typically syrups flavored with fruits and herbs and paired with water, cocktails, or seltzer. In North America, cordials are better known as alcohol-based infusions of various plants that are usually sweet, bitter, or spicy. While there are recipes for both types of cordials in this book, the primary focus is on alcohol-based infusions, the sort of cordials that are meant to be sipped on to promote good health and good fun. However, I also include a chapter on medicinal and fruit-based syrups, so don't fret, I've got you covered.

Cordials can be a beautiful way to indulge in your favorite spirit while remaining in touch with your herbal allies. That being said, there is a time and a place for such beauty and magic. Alcohol has set its grasp on many, sometimes inflicting more harm than pleasure. The cordials in this book are meant to be taken and enjoyed in small doses. Keep a steady hand when pouring these drinks as they are powerful and medicinal.

Terms, Tools & Tricks

Cordial: A sweet or pleasant-tasting liquor

Macerate: To infuse food or herbs into a liquid

Muddle: To crush up ingredients in order to release essential oils and flavors

Helpful Tools

- Mason jars of all sizes
- Decorative bottles to store cordials, shrubs, etc.
- Tinted dropper bottles to store bitters, syrups, etc.
- Fine-mesh strainer or Hawthorne cocktail strainer
- Cheesecloth or muslin
- Muddler
- Funnel

Most of the cordial recipes in this book are meant to be made in pint-size jars and therefore will call for 2 cups wine or another spirit. If you wish to make them in a quart jar, simply double the amount called for in each recipe.

2 cups = 1 pint
4 cups = 1 quart

Fresh herbs and flowers typically take less time to infuse than dried herbs when making a cordial, because flavors tend to be most potent when a plant is fresh. This also applies to fruits and vegetables.

Infusion time can vary from one night to one year! It really depends on your taste preference, so do little taste tests whenever you feel inclined. Strength increases over time.

Cordials will keep for up to two years and often longer if stored in a cupboard with a properly capped bottle or jar. Store infused wines in the fridge for longer use.

Trust your intuition when making a cordial. If you feel called to add more or less of something or to make substitutions, then go for it! There is so much magic in medicine making, and learning to listen to the plants you feel drawn to makes the process much more personal and powerful.

Keep your infusions in a cool, dark place, like a cupboard or on a shelf that does not receive sunlight. Make sure to give them a good shake daily.

Store cordials, syrups, and other herbal creations in clean jars or bottles. Mason jars are my go-to. Thrift stores often have a good selection of vintage bottles and jars that are also suited for storage of cordials and syrups. And they make great gifts! Just make sure all your jars or bottles have secure caps.

When it comes to the quality of the spirit I use to make a cordial, I don't usually spend my money on organic or super high-quality alcohol. The herbs will often mask the flavor of the actual liquor or wine, making it difficult to judge what you paid for it. On a certain level, cheap vodka is cheap vodka, and if you have the means to purchase organic liquor, it won't hurt. But I'm not one to preach the importance of using expensive products when making cordials, having spent quite a few years of my life on a strict budget. If you put enough love, plants, and soul into your cordial making process, no one will be able to taste the difference.

Straining Equipment

- ⚘ Fine-mesh strainer
- ⚘ Hawthorne cocktail strainer
- ⚘ Cheesecloth or muslin

Strain your cordials into a clean bowl through any of the above tools. Clean the original infusion jar before transferring the strained concoction back in or grab a new bottle and transfer the liquid to that. Cover tightly and store in the fridge or cupboard.

Disclaimer

These recipes are meant to be consumed
with joy and positive intention. Please drink with care and
consideration for yourself and the plants.

Plants are powerful, and so are you.

Spring

LILAC WINE

For when the heart aches

+ 2-3 Fresh lilac sprigs
+ 3 tablespoons honey
+ 2 cups white wine
+ 1 rose quartz crystal (optional)

Remove the petals from the lilac stems & place them in a pint-sized jar. Add the honey, drop in the crystal, and cover with wine. Cap tightly and infuse for 3-4 days, shaking daily.

Serve chilled on its own or with champagne or seltzer. Store up to 1 month in the fridge.

DOUGLAS FIR TIPSY

- 1 cup Douglas fir tips
- 1/2 cup chopped crystallized ginger
- 2 cinnamon sticks
- 2 cups vodka or gin

Place the dry ingredients in a pint-size jar and cover with vodka. Cap tightly and infuse for 4 to 8 weeks, shaking daily.

- Serve chilled with tonic water and a sprig of thyme. Store for up to 6 months in the fridge or cupboard.

13

SOOTHE YOURSELF TONIC

- 1/4 cup lemon balm
- 1/4 cup rose petals
- 1/4 cup tulsi (holy basil)
- 1 tablespoon chamomile
- 2 cups sweet white wine, such as Riesling or Moscato

Place the dry ingredients in a pint-size jar and cover with the wine. Cap tightly and infuse for 2 to 3 weeks, shaking daily.

Store up to one month in the fridge.

LOVERS' LIP

A libation for 1, 2 or few

+ 1/4 cup damiana
+ 1/4 cup rose hips
+ 1/4 cup rose petals
+ 1/4 cup fresh or dried elderflower
+ 2 cups white wine

Place the dry ingredients in a pint-size jar and cover with the wine. Cap tightly and infuse for 1-2 weeks, shaking daily.

Serve chilled. Store for up to 2 months in the fridge.

OH MARY!

A Bloody Mary base

◊ 5 to 7 dill sprigs, chopped
◊ 2 garlic cloves, crushed
◊ 3 cocktail onions
◊ 1 tablespoon peppercorns
◊ 1 hot pepper of your choice, sliced (optional)
◊ 2 cups vodka

Place the dill & garlic in a quart-size jar. Add remaining ingredients and cover with vodka. Cap tightly and infuse for 3-5 days, shaking daily.

Serve with tomato juice, gray salt, horseradish, Worcestershire sauce, and lemon wedges. Store for up to 6 months in the fridge or cupboard.

17

CHAMPAGNE STRAWBERRIES

A bubbly berry for your
cocktail or cordial

- 2 cups hulled strawberries
- 1 small bunch fresh mint
  or tulsi (holy basil)
  leaves
- one 750 ml bottle
  sparkling wine

Place the strawberries and mint
or tulsi in a wide-mouth quart-size
jar and cover with the wine. Infuse
overnight in fridge.

TULSI ME TULSI

- ◆ 1/4 cup tulsi (holy basil)
- ◆ 1/4 cup rose petals
- ◆ 1/4 cup violets
- ◆ 1/4 cup sugar
- ◆ 2 cups vodka

Place ingredients in a pint-size jar and cover with vodka. Cap tightly and shake. Infuse for 2 to 4 weeks, shaking daily.

Serve chilled with elderflower syrup (page 61) and sparkling wine or seltzer. Store for up to 6 months in the fridge or cupboard.

DANDELION SWAG

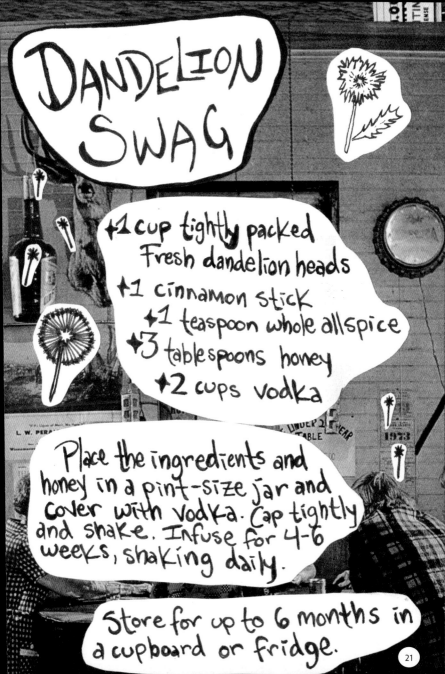

- 1 cup tightly packed fresh dandelion heads
- 1 cinnamon stick
- 1 teaspoon whole allspice
- 3 tablespoons honey
- 2 cups vodka

Place the ingredients and honey in a pint-size jar and cover with vodka. Cap tightly and shake. Infuse for 4-6 weeks, shaking daily.

Store for up to 6 months in a cupboard or fridge.

21

Summer

BLACKBERRY GIN·GER

- ◊ 6 ounces blackberries
- ◊ 1/4 cup chopped crystallized ginger
- ◊ 1 heaping tablespoon lavender
- ◊ 2 cups gin

Muddle the blackberries in a pint-size jar. Add remaining dry ingredients and cover with gin. Cap tightly and shake. Infuse for 3 to 6 weeks, shaking daily.

Store for up to 6 months in the fridge or cupboard.

CARMELITE WATER

First created in the sixteenth century by Carmelite monks in Switzerland, Carmelite water can be used to treat nervous headaches & to ease digestive upset.

◊ 1/4 cup fresh or dried lemon balm
◊ 1/4 cup dried angelica root
◊ Pinch of freshly grated nutmeg
◊ 1-2 sweet marjoram sprigs
◊ 2 cups sweet white wine

Place ingredients in a pint-size jar and cover with wine. Infuse for 2-6 weeks, shaking daily.

Store for up to 1 month in the fridge or cupboard.

DRUNK IN LOVE

◊ 1 jalapeño, seeded & sliced
◊ 1/2 cup seeded, cubed watermelon
◊ 1 tablespoon agave
◊ 2 cups white tequila

Muddle the peppers in a pint-sized jar. Add the watermelon and agave and cover with tequila. Infuse for 3 to 6 weeks, shaking daily.

Serve chilled. Store up to 6 months in the fridge or cupboard.

SOMMARVATTEN

"summer water"

- ✧ 1 cup strawberries, hulled and sliced
- ✧ 2 tablespoons elderflower
- ✧ 2 tablespoons calendula
- ✧ 2 tablespoons agave
- ✧ 2 cups rosé wine

Muddle the strawberries in a pint-size jar then add dry ingredients. Add the agave & cover with rosé. Cap tightly & infuse for 1 week, shaking daily.

Serve chilled. Store up to 1 month in the fridge.

AVONLEA RASPBERRY CORDIAL

- ◊ 6 ounces raspberries
- ◊ 1/4 cup red raspberry leaves
- ◊ 1 cup sugar
- ◊ 2 cups vodka

Fresh or dry

Muddle the raspberries & raspberry leaves in a pint-size jar. Add the sugar & cover with vodka. Cap tightly and shake. Infuse for 6-8 weeks, shaking daily.

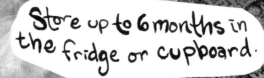

Store up to 6 months in the fridge or cupboard.

HABANERO HERO

- ◇ 2 habanero peppers, seeded & sliced
- ◇ 1 rosemary sprig
- ◇ ½ small grapefruit, thinly sliced with the peel left on
- ◇ 2 cups gold tequila

Muddle the pepper slices and rosemary in a pint-size jar. Add grapefruit slices and cover with tequila. Cap tightly and shake. Infuse for 3-6 weeks, shaking daily.

Store for up to 6 months in the fridge or cupboard.

White Wine versus Red

You may have noticed that a lot of the wine-based recipes in this book call for white wine. I don't often use red wine when making cordials, partly because I'm a purist when it comes to a good Chianti or Cabernet and partly because red wines tend to have a fuller, more complex flavor, which often masks the taste of floral plants and lighter herbs. Unless an infusion is being served hot and spicy, like Glögg (page 52), I typically don't make cordials with red wine. However, when I do use a red, I like to pair it with berries, roots, and mushrooms due to their earthy nature.

When we first discussed cordial making at herb school, one of my teachers suggested that white wine is best for herbal infusions because of its "emptiness." While white wines are certainly flavorful, their flavors tend to be more malleable than reds'. There is a sense that there is room within a white wine for embellishment,

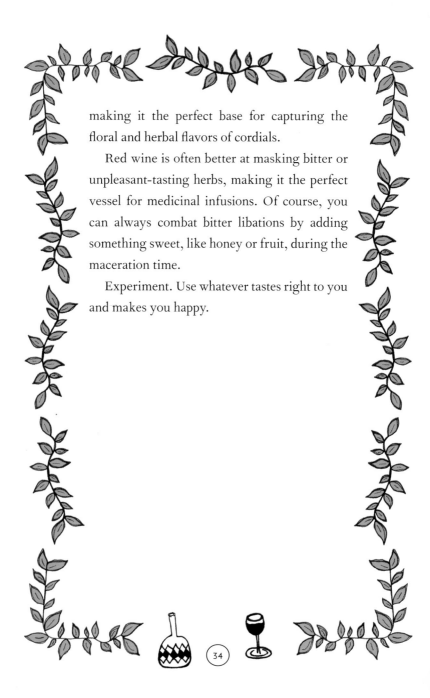

making it the perfect base for capturing the floral and herbal flavors of cordials.

Red wine is often better at masking bitter or unpleasant-tasting herbs, making it the perfect vessel for medicinal infusions. Of course, you can always combat bitter libations by adding something sweet, like honey or fruit, during the maceration time.

Experiment. Use whatever tastes right to you and makes you happy.

Autumn

ELDERBERRY BREW

- ♢ 2 slices orange, peel left on
- ♢ 1/4 cup elderberries
- ♢ 1/4 cup red raspberry leaves
- ♢ 4 tablespoons agave
- ♢ 2 cups Mezcal

Place the orange slices in a pint-size jar, standing them upright against the walls of the jar. Add the elderberries, red raspberry leaves & agave & cover with mezcal. Infuse for 4-6 weeks, shaking daily.

Store for up to 6 months in cupboard or fridge.

ORANGE YOU GLAD I DIDN'T SAY CLOVE?

- ✩ 1/2 orange, peeled
- ✩ 1 teaspoon whole cloves
- ✩ 1 cinnamon stick
- ✩ 1/4 cup sliced almonds
- ✩ 1/2 cup coconut sugar
- ✩ 2 cups rum

Muddle the orange & almonds in a pint-size jar. Add remaining ingredients & cover with rum. Cap tightly and shake. Infuse for 4-6 weeks, shaking daily.

Store for up to 6 months in fridge or cupboard.

CHAI BABY

- ◊ 1/2 cup sliced peeled ginger
- ◊ 2 cinnamon sticks
- ◊ 1 tablespoon cardamom
- ◊ 1 teaspoon peppercorns
- ◊ 1/2 teaspoon whole cloves
- ◊ 2 tablespoons maple syrup
- ◊ 2 cups apple brandy

Muddle the ginger in a pint-size jar. Add remaining ingredients and cover with the apple brandy. Infuse for 4-6 weeks, shaking daily.

Combine with apple cider or Golden Milk (page 99), or make a fancy hot toddy with your favorite tea & lots of honey. Store for up to 6 months in the fridge or cupboard.

PLUM DRUNK

- ✦ 1 cup pitted plums
- ✦ 1/2 cup raw sugar
- ✦ 1/2 cup chamomile
- ✦ 1 vanilla bean, sliced lengthwise
- ✦ 2 cups brandy

Place the ingredients in a pint-size jar. Cap tightly and shake. Infuse for 6-8 weeks, shaking daily.

Store up to 6 months in the fridge or cupboard.

BEETS ME

- 1 cup diced peeled beets
- 2 tablespoons grated peeled ginger
- 1 tablespoon peppercorns
- 2 cups brandy

Place the ingredients in a pint-size jar and cover with brandy. Cap tightly and shake. Infuse for 3-5 weeks, shaking daily.

Store for up to 6 months in the fridge or cupboard.

41

HEART HEALER

for emotional strength of heart

- ✦ 1/2 cup fresh or dried hawthorn berries
- ✦ 2 cinnamon sticks
- ✦ 1 vanilla bean, sliced lengthwise
- ✦ 1 teaspoon whole allspice
- ✦ 2 tablespoons pure maple syrup
- ✦ 2 cups red wine

Place dry ingredients in a pint-size jar and cover with wine. Cap tightly and shake. Infuse for 2-3 weeks, shaking daily.

Store for up to 2 months in a cupboard.

Winter

CINNAPOMME

- ♢ 1/2 large pear, cut into small cubes
- ♢ 1 tablespoon golden raisins
- ♢ 3 cinnamon sticks
- ♢ 1 tablespoon whole allspice
- ♢ 2 cups apple whiskey

Muddle the pear cubes & raisins in a pint-size jar. Add the cinnamon sticks & allspice & cover with whiskey. Infuse for 4 to 6 weeks, shaking daily.

Store for up to 6 months in a cupboard.

DIGESTIVE BRANDY

◇ 1/2 cup fennel seeds
◇ 1/4 cup fresh or dried wormwood
◇ 3 star anise
◇ 2-3 tablespoons honey
◇ 2 cups brandy

Muddle the fennel seeds in a pint-size jar. Add remaining ingredients and cover with brandy. Cap tightly and shake. Infuse for 6-8 weeks, shaking daily.

Serve in 1-ounce glasses before or after a meal. Store for up to 6 months in a cupboard.

REISHI RED

For strength of heart, body, and mind.

- ☆ 1/4 cup rosehips
- ☆ 8 thin slices reishi mushroom
- ☆ 2 tablespoons ashwagandha root
- ☆ 1/2 cup honey
- ☆ 2 cups red wine

Muddle rose hips in a pint-size jar. Add remaining ingredients and cover with wine. Cap tightly and shake. Infuse for 3-5 weeks, shaking daily.

Store for up to 2 months in the fridge or cupboard

THE LONG SLEEP AFTER

Invigorating aphrodisiac elixir
and sleep aid

◊ 2 tablespoons grated peeled ginger
◊ 1/4 cup damiana
◊ 2 tablespoons dried rose petals
◊ 2 tablespoons Milky oats or oat straw
◊ 1/2 cup coconut sugar
◊ 1 vanilla bean, sliced lengthwise
◊ 2 cups vodka or brandy

Place the dry ingredients in a pint-size jar & cover with vodka or brandy. Infuse for 4-6 weeks, shaking daily.

Store for up to 6 months in a cupboard.

SASSY PANTS

- ✧ 1 cup stemmed, pitted cherries
- ✧ 1/4 cup rose hips
- ✧ 3 tablespoons dried sassafras
- ✧ 1 to 2 tablespoons honey
- ✧ 2 cups white wine

Root & bark

Muddle the cherries & rose hips in a pint-size jar. Add sassafras & honey & cover with wine. Cap tightly & shake. Infuse for 5-7 weeks, shaking daily.

Store for up to one month in the fridge.

51

GLÖGG

A Swedish holiday staple.
God Jul!

A two-part recipe

- 3 small oranges, peeled
- 1 cup raisins
- 1 1/2 cups sliced almonds
- 3 tablespoons cardamom
- 5 cinnamon sticks
- 2 tablespoons whole cloves
- One 750 ml bottle port wine
- One 750 ml bottle red wine
- 1 pint vodka or brandy
- Sugar or honey for sweetening (optional)

✦ Muddle the oranges, raisins & almonds in a bowl then transfer to a half-gallon-size jar. Add remaining dry ingredients and cover with port. Cap tightly & shake. Label & infuse for 2-4 weeks, shaking daily.

After infusion time, pour the mixture into a large pot on the stove over low heat. Add the red wine and vodka and let simmer for 25-30 minutes. Taste and add a bit of sugar or honey, if desired, for more sweetness. Strain and serve hot.

Store for up to 2 days in the fridge.

A DREAMER'S CORDIAL

To encourage & enhance deep dreams

- ✦ 1/4 cup mugwort
- ✦ 2 tablespoons damiana
- ✦ 2 cinnamon sticks
- ✦ 1/2 cup honey
- ✦ 2 cups red wine

Place the dry ingredients & honey in a pint-size jar and cover with wine. Cap tightly & shake. Infuse for 2 to 4 weeks, shaking daily.

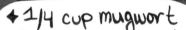

Store for up to 2 months in the cupboard.

Drink 1 to 2 ounces before bed.

Sweeteners

There are a number of ways to sweeten a cordial, and what you use should depend on your taste preference. Each spirit will adjust to a given sweetener in its own way, so I suggest that you play around with different sugars. Fruits are often an excellent way to naturally sweeten your cordials. By adding fruit to the jar and muddling it, you are releasing sugars and flavor that can really embellish your infusion. Dry fruits tend to have a higher sugar content and are easy to keep on hand for year-round cordial making. However, making a cordial with fresh fruit is a beautiful method of preservation and a good way to keep in touch with different seasons as they come and go.

 Sweet Ideas

- Agave
- Sugar
- Honey
- Maple syrup
- Fruit
- Coconut sugar

Keep in mind that you can always substitute one sweetener for another with any of the recipes in this book.

Syrups

Syrups are an incredible way to incorporate herbs into your daily life. They are sweet, flavorful, and effective when used correctly. Syrups are one of my favorite ways to get my herbal dosage, and the palatable nature of syrups makes it easy for folks with stubborn taste buds to get theirs as well. Plus, a syrup's medicinal content can be disguised and passed off as an exciting new kind of soda or cocktail.

The possibilities of what you can do with syrups are endless: ingest them by the spoonful, add them to fizzy water, soak a cake in them, mix them with milky coffees and teas, or use them as the base for a badass mocktail. There is no wrong way to use a syrup.

Syrups can keep for up to three months in the fridge and even longer if there's an added preservative, like brandy, in the mix. Brandy can also make the syrup more shelf/counter stable if the mix is bottled and stored properly. I typically add about ¼ cup brandy per 1 cup syrup. This will, of course, affect the taste of your syrup, so you may want to add a bit more sweetener to offset the taste of the liquor. Always keep your syrups out of direct sunlight or in the fridge to prevent mold growth.

Store syrups in pint- or quart-size mason jars (or whatever you have on hand). Keep a piece of wax paper or cloth between the jar and lid to prevent sticking. Pop-top or antique bottles work as well and are a nice way to present a syrup, especially if you are giving it as a gift.

Summer Berry and Schizandra Syrup

from Summer & Sarah of the Great Kosmic Kitchen

- ✧ 4 cups raspberries
- ✧ Juice of 1/2 lemon
- ✧ 1 tablespoon dried schizandra
- ✧ 1/2 tablespoon dried rosepetals
- ✧ 1 cup honey, plus more if needed

In a large, heavy-bottomed saucepan, bring to a boil the raspberries, lemon juice, and 1 cup water. Reduce the heat to a simmer and add the schizandra and rose petals. Let simmer for 15 to 20 minutes or until the berries have broken down. Remove from the heat and let cool.

Strain the mixture into a large bowl. Stir in the honey, adding more if needed to get a syrupy consistency. Pour the syrup through a funnel into a jar or bottles, cap tightly, and label. Store for up to 3 months in the fridge.

Elderflower Syrup
-Fläderblomssaft-

♦ 2 pounds sugar
♦ 20 to 25 fresh elderflower heads
♦ 1 1/2 lemons, sliced
♦ 1 ounce citric acid

In a large saucepan over medium heat, dissolve the sugar in 4½ cups water. Place the elderflowers, lemon slices, and citric acid in a large heat-proof container. Pour the hot sugar water over the flowers and lemons and stir well. Cover with a cloth or lid and let rest on a countertop for 3 to 4 days.

Strain the mixture into a jar or bottles, cap tightly, and label. Store for up to 3 months in the fridge.

Reishi & Elderberry Syrup

- ✧ **1 cup** elderberries
- ✧ **8 to 10** slices reishi mushroom
- ✧ **3** cinnamon sticks
- ✧ **1** tablespoon cardamom
- ✧ **1½** cups honey

In a medium saucepan, bring to a boil the elderberries, mushroom slices, cinnamon sticks, cardamom, and 3 cups water. Reduce heat to low and let simmer for 25 to 30 minutes, or until the liquid has reduced by about ½ cup.

Strain the mixture into a large bowl. While still hot, stir in the honey until dissolved. Let the syrup cool, then pour it through a funnel into a jar or bottles, cap tightly, and label. Store for up to 3 months in the fridge.

Soothing Syrup

-To calm the nerves-

♦ 6 slices reishi mushroom
♦ 1/2 cup dried tulsi (holy basil)
♦ 1/4 cup dried linden
♦ 1/4 cup dried rose petals
♦ 1 cup honey
♦ 1/2 teaspoon vanilla extract

In a medium saucepan, bring to a boil the mushroom slices and 3 cups water. Reduce the heat to low and add the tulsi, linden, and rose petals. Cover and let simmer for 20 to 25 minutes, or until the liquid has reduced by about ½ cup.

Strain the mixture into a large bowl. While still hot, stir in the honey until dissolved and add the vanilla extract. Let the syrup cool, then pour it through a funnel into a jar or bottles, cap tightly, and label. Store for up to 3 months in the fridge.

Forest Path

A conifer syrup by Milla Prince
of The Woman Who Married a Bear

- ◆1 cup conifer tips, spruce or fir
- ◆1 cup honey

Harvested in Spring

In a large saucepan over medium heat, bring to a simmer the tips and 3 cups water, stirring as they cook. It's important to keep the water below the boiling point in order to preserve vitamins and other medicinal constituents. Continue simmering until the liquid has reduced by about ½ cup, 20 to 25 minutes.

Strain the mixture into a large bowl. Stir in the honey. (It's up to you how sweet you want to make it, but 1 cup honey will make this the strength of commonly used simple syrups; if you prefer it less sweet, ½ cup will work.) Let cool, then pour the syrup through a funnel into a jar or bottles, cap tightly, and label. Store for up to 3 months in the fridge.

Milla suggests combining 1 teaspoon conifer syrup with 2 ounces gin, fizzy water, and a splash of orange juice. "You'll beat any summer cold in no time, while keeping cool as a cucumber—or a conifer!"

Dandelion & Ginger Syrup

◇ **2** cups fresh dandelion heads
◇ **1** cup chopped peeled ginger
◇ Juice of 1|2 lemon
◇ **2** cups raw sugar or honey

Remove the green sepals from the base of the dandelion heads; these greens are bitter and will affect the sweetness of the syrup.

In a large saucepan, bring to a boil 1 cup of the dandelions, the ginger, lemon juice, and 3 cups water. Reduce the heat to low, add the remaining 1 cup dandelions, and simmer for 10 to 15 minutes, or until the liquid has reduced by ½ cup.

Strain the mixture into a large bowl. While still hot, stir in the sugar until dissolved. Let the syrup cool, then pour it through a funnel into a jar or bottles, cap tightly, and label. Store for up to 3 months in the fridge.

Shrubs

If you're anything like me, you may find yourself over-whelmed with the seemingly endless selection of produce at the market during spring and summer. If I can't fit everything in my shopping basket, I'll often mentally note to return within the next few days to pick up the one seasonal fruit or vegetable that didn't make it in with my weekly produce. Flash-forward to two weeks later when I finally make it back, only to discover that the fruit I previously wanted is already well out of season. One of my go-to methods for solving this revolving door of seasonal foods is to make a shrub. Shrubs, also known as drinking vinegars, have a long history of use in cultures around the world. Before refrigeration, shrubs were a valuable method of preserving fresh fruits, flowers, and herbs. Vinegar, a main ingredient in shrubs, is an incredible preservative due to its high content of acetic acid, which kills microbes and prevents food from spoiling.

How to Use Shrubs

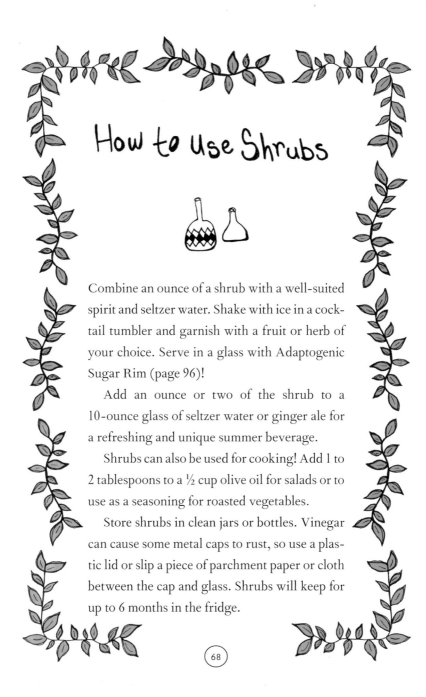

Combine an ounce of a shrub with a well-suited spirit and seltzer water. Shake with ice in a cocktail tumbler and garnish with a fruit or herb of your choice. Serve in a glass with Adaptogenic Sugar Rim (page 96)!

Add an ounce or two of the shrub to a 10-ounce glass of seltzer water or ginger ale for a refreshing and unique summer beverage.

Shrubs can also be used for cooking! Add 1 to 2 tablespoons to a ½ cup olive oil for salads or to use as a seasoning for roasted vegetables.

Store shrubs in clean jars or bottles. Vinegar can cause some metal caps to rust, so use a plastic lid or slip a piece of parchment paper or cloth between the cap and glass. Shrubs will keep for up to 6 months in the fridge.

Blueberry, lavender & Fig

- 2 cups sugar
- 1 cup figs, stemmed and quartered
- 1 cup blueberries
- 1/2 cup dried lavender
- 3 cups red wine vinegar

In a large saucepan over medium heat, stir the sugar into 2 cups water until dissolved. Add the figs, blueberries, and lavender to the sugar water. Simmer until the fruit breaks down and the syrup is the same color as the fruit, about 15 minutes. Add the vinegar and simmer for another 5 minutes.

Strain the mixture into a large bowl. Let the shrub cool, then pour it through a funnel into a quart-size jar or bottles and cap tightly. Label and store for up to 6 months in the fridge.

Apple, Rose & Hawthorn

♦ 1 1/2 cups honey
♦ 2 medium apples, peeled, cored, and cubed
♦ 2 cups fresh rose petals or 1 cup dried
♦ 1 cup hawthorn berries
♦ 2 cups raw apple cider vinegar

In a large saucepan over medium heat, stir the honey into 2 cups water until dissolved. Add the apples, rose petals, and hawthorn berries to the sweetened water. Simmer until the apples and berries break down and the syrup is the same color as the fruit, about 15 minutes. Add the vinegar and simmer for another 5 minutes.

Strain the mixture into a large bowl. Let the shrub cool, then pour it through a funnel into a jar or bottles and cap tightly. Label and store for up to 6 months in the fridge.

Blood Orange & Spruce Tip

◊ 1 1/2 cups fresh spruce tips (harvested in spring)
  ◊ 2 blood oranges, sliced
  ◊ 1 tablespoon whole allspice
   ◊ 3 cinnamon sticks
   ◊ 2 cups raw sugar
   ◊ 3 cups raw apple cider vinegar

Place the spruce tips, oranges, allspice, cinnamon, and sugar in a widemouthed half-gallon-size jar and cover with the vinegar. Place a square of parchment paper between the lid and the jar, cap tightly, and shake. Place in the fridge and infuse for 5 to 6 days, shaking daily.

Strain the mixture into a jar or bottles, cap tightly, and label. Store for up to 6 months in the fridge.

Other Combinations to Consider

PEACHES + ROOIBOS TEA + RAW SUGAR + CHAMPAGNE VINEGAR

BEETS + PEPPERCORN + HONEY + RED WINE VINEGAR

STRAWBERRIES + LEMON BALM + RAW SUGAR + WHITE WINE VINEGAR

BLACKBERRIES + CHERRIES + CINNAMON + RED WINE VINEGAR

Bitters

I'm not exaggerating when I say that bitters changed my life. My first experience with a bitters blend was at herb school in 2013, and I will admit that it was not love at first taste. Bitters are exactly that—bitter and not terribly kind to the taste buds. However, after a few days of ingesting my new bitters blend first thing in the morning and before each meal, I was hooked. My digestion had improved and I no longer felt bogged down after meals or hit with a sudden bout of bloat. Bitters had saved me and I became an advocate for bitter plants all over the world. I became the person at the dinner table passing around a little brown bottle of bitters while trying to convince my nonherbalist friends that the pungent-tasting liquid I was doling out actually had health benefits. I hung mugwort from my car's rearview mirror and plucked artichoke leaves from gardens while walking through my sleepy California town. I once went to a party with a friend and sat on a couch in the corner while nervously chewing on milk thistle seeds—eating each bitter little morsel one by one. I think it's safe to say I was not the life of the party that night, but at least my digestion was on point.

Bitters are not historically a big part of North American cuisine, but they are quickly finding their place at the table and in our glasses. When it comes to cocktails, there seems to be a huge resurgence of new bitters formulas appearing on shelves across the country. I've found many books devoted solely to the topic of bitters, and it's hard to find a cocktail bar that doesn't make its own blends or carry a variety of different brands.

Bitter plants aid the digestive system by stimulating the production of bile stored in the gallbladder and improving liver function. Hold bitters on or under your tongue for five to ten seconds when taking them in tincture form. The bitter taste of the plant is essential to the digestive process and letting it sit on your tongue will jump-start that process.

For the sake of strength and extraction of herbs, I recommend the use of Everclear, which is a corn-based 190-proof alcohol. If you prefer to skip the Everclear, or if it isn't available to you, substitute with a standard 80-proof vodka.

Store bitters in tinted bottles with dropper tops. Add a dropperful or two of bitters blend to a cocktail or take on its own to aid digestion. The following recipes are meant to be consumed in small doses (i.e., by the dropperful).

Orange Peel, Gentian Root & Sassafras

◊ 3/4 cup fresh orange peel
◊ 1/4 cup gentian root
◊ 1/2 cup sassafras
◊ 2 tablespoons pure maple syrup
◊ 1 cup Everclear
◊ 2 cups rum

Place the orange peel, gentian, sassafras, and maple syrup in a quart-size jar and cover with the Everclear and rum. Cap tightly and shake. Place in the cupboard and infuse for 2 weeks, shaking daily.

Strain the mixture into a clean jar and funnel into dropper bottles as needed. Store for up to 1 year in the cupboard.

Cherry & Cardamom

◊ **1** ½ cups stemmed, pitted cherries
◊ **4** tablespoons cardamom
◊ **2** tablespoons honey
◊ **1** cup Everclear
◊ **2** cups Brandy

Place the cherries, cardamom, and honey in a quart-size jar and cover with the Everclear and brandy. Cap tightly and shake. Place in the cupboard and infuse for 2 weeks, shaking daily.

Strain the mixture into a clean jar and funnel into dropper bottles as needed. Store for up to 1 year in the cupboard.

Ginger, Chamomile & Rose

◇ **1** cup thinly sliced peeled ginger
◇ 1/2 cup chamomile
◇ **1**/2 cup rose petals
◇ **2** tablespoons honey
◇ **1** cup Everclear
◇ **2** cups brandy

Muddle the ginger in a quart-size jar. Add the chamomile, rose petals, and honey and cover with the Everclear and brandy. Cap tightly and shake. Place in the cupboard and infuse for 2 weeks, shaking daily.

Strain the mixture into a clean jar and funnel into dropper bottles as needed. Store for up to 1 year in the cupboard.

Blood Orange, Thyme & Peppercorn

◊ 1 blood orange, cut into cubes with peel left on
◊ 6 to 8 fresh thyme sprigs
◊ 1/2 tablespoon whole peppercorns
◊ 3 tablespoons agave
◊ 1 cup Everclear
◊ 2 cups white tequila

Muddle the orange, thyme, and peppercorns in a quart-size jar. Add the agave and cover with the Everclear and tequila. Cap tightly and shake. Place in the cupboard and infuse for 2 weeks, shaking daily.

Strain the mixture into a clean jar and funnel into dropper bottles as needed. Store for up to 1 year in the cupboard.

Other Bitter Herbs
to Consider

ARTICHOKE LEAF
DANDELION ROOT & LEAF
GOLDENSEAL
HOPS
LAVENDER
MILK THISTLE
MUGWORT
WORMWOOD
YARROW

Materia Medica

Materia medica is the collection of plants and other substances that are used in the practice of herbal medicine. The plants in this chapter are meant to enhance herbal wisdom and knowledge. Use Herbal Actions: A Glossary of Terms on page 109 to find definitions for the terms used in the remedial-use descriptions below.

The plants and remedies in this book are meant to inspire, not treat, cure, or prevent ailments. Always consult an herbalist or other practitioner before beginning a new herbal regimen.

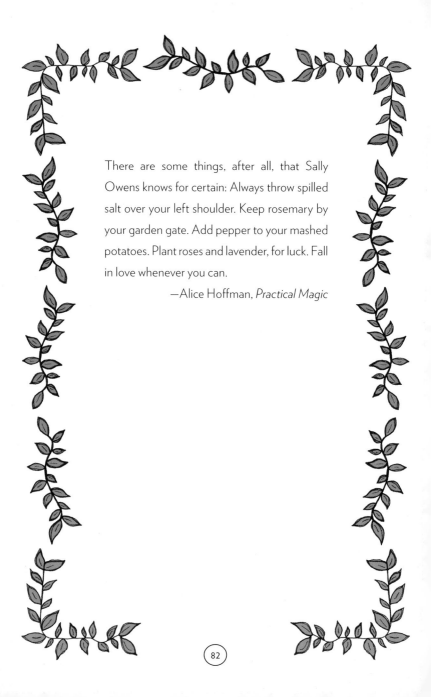

There are some things, after all, that Sally Owens knows for certain: Always throw spilled salt over your left shoulder. Keep rosemary by your garden gate. Add pepper to your mashed potatoes. Plant roses and lavender, for luck. Fall in love whenever you can.

—Alice Hoffman, *Practical Magic*

Chamomile
Matricaria chamomilla

Parts Used: Flowers

Remedial Uses: Anodyne, tonic, nervine, antispasmodic, astringent, carminative

History & Lore: Historical use of chamomile dates back to the ancient Egyptians. It was once used as an offering to the sun and is associated with the sun god Ra.

The word *chamomile* is derived from the Greek word *khamaimēlon*, which means "earth apple," due to chamomile's apple-like scent.

Chamomile has many uses. It can help overcome feelings of anger and grief. It is used as a hair rinse to enhance the color of blond hair. It is also said to bring health to surrounding plants in a garden. Plant chamomile near other plants that are tricky to grow. A bath drawn with chamomile will attract love and prosperity.

Dandelion

Taraxacum officinale

Parts Used: Flowers, leaves, and roots

Remedial Uses: Diuretic, tonic, nutrient, bitter, mild laxative

History & Lore: Dandelion is considered to be a survivor, thanks to its resilient growing patterns. Those survivor energetics can be transmitted to humans through consumption and appreciation of these powerful little weeds.

When roasted, the roots make a fine coffee substitute, especially when mixed with reishi or chicory root. While dandelion flowers are somewhat sweet and well suited for cordials and syrups, the young leaves are bitter and make an excellent addition to salads and stir-fries.

In French, dandelions are called *dent-de-lion*, which translates to "tooth of the lion."

Elder

Sambucus nigra

Parts Used: Flowers and berries

Remedial Uses: Expectorant, demulcent, diaphoretic, antiviral

History & Lore: It was once common for people to hide among the elder trees during Midsummer nights to catch glimpses of faeries.

Elderberry syrup is a common aid to prevent and treat colds and flu. While the base of this syrup is the elderberry, the flowers can also be added to other syrups as a flavor. See recipe for Reishi & Elderberry Syrup on page 62. An old folk remedy uses the leaves of the elderberry tree to topically treat sprains and bruises.

The branches of the elder tree contain a light pith that is easily removed and can be hollowed out to make flutes.

The berries bloom in late summer. They are quite popular with birds, so get to them quickly (but make sure to leave enough for our feathered friends).

Ginger
Zingiber officinale

Parts Used: Root

Remedial Uses: Carminative, emmenagogue, diaphoretic, anti-inflammatory

History & Lore: Ginger has been cultivated and used as a medicinal herb in China for over five thousand years. It is said to enhance energy before magical practice. In Ayurvedic medicine, ginger is known to be beneficial for all doshas (vata, pitta, kapha) but especially kapha as it sparks energy. The word *ginger* derives from the Sanskrit word *singabera*, which means horn-shaped.

Ginger's warming properties work well for the treatment of cramps. Make a poultice by grinding up peeled fresh ginger and placing it on skin. For menstrual cramps, roll freshly minced ginger into a ball and place in belly button.

Holy Basil (Tulsi)

Ocimum tenuiflorum

Parts Used: Leaves

Remedial Uses: Adaptogen, aromatic, carminative, nervine, demulcent

History & Lore: Tulsi is celebrated in Hindu tradition and considered to be a most sacred plant. It is associated with the goddess Tulsi, who is closely connected to Vishnu. No ritual is complete without the presence of tulsi.

It is a Hindu tradition to have a tulsi plant growing near or in front of your home for protection and luck. Tulsi bead necklaces (made from the wood of the plant) are worn around the neck to prevent bad dreams, physical attacks, and accidents.

Tulsi is a powerful herb for enhancing emotional well-being. Brew into tea with rose petals to ease anxiety, or simply sit with the plant itself to enjoy its restorative effects.

Lavender
Lavandula officinalis

Parts Used: Flowers

Remedial Uses: Nervine, carminative, aromatic, antifungal, vulnerary, analgesic

History & Lore: Lavender is known to bring luck, happiness, and relaxation. Lavender can be burned and used as a magical smudge to promote sleep and sweet dreams.

It is traditional for brides in Ireland to place sprigs of lavender, a symbol of love and devotion, in their bouquets. More practically, sachets of dried lavender flowers placed in closets and dresser drawers keep moths away.

Lemon Balm
Melissa officinalis

Parts Used: Leaves

Remedial Uses: Aromatic, adaptogen, nervine, antispasmodic, carminative, shen tonic

History & Lore: "Causeth the heart and mind to become merry."
—Nicholas Culpeper

Lemon balm is said to be ruled by the planet Jupiter and Cancer, the zodiac sign that is bound to water and associated with emotional health. Lemon balm has long been known to remedy emotional distress, be it anxiety, nervousness, or heartache. It is used in Ayurvedic medicine to ease stomach upsets. Lemon balm is often used in ceremonies and is worn to attract a lover.

Harvest lemon balm on Midsummer morning and throw last year's harvest into the fire come Midsummer nightfall.

Mugwort

Artemisia vulgaris

Parts Used: Leaves and roots

Remedial Uses: Diuretic, emmenagogue, abortifacient, nervine, aromatic

History & Lore: Perhaps the herb most commonly associated with ceremony and magic, mugwort can be used in a number of ways: keep under a pillow for heavy dreams, burn dry in a room or during sacred practice, or add to a smoke blend.

Mugwort's Latin name is derived from Artemis, the Olympian goddess of hunting, wilderness, and childbirth. Because of its affinity to the uterus, it has a long history of use by women. It has been known to bring about delayed menstruation and restore monthly cycles. Harvest during daylight hours when the moon is full.

Raspberry Leaf

Rubusidaeus idaeus

Parts Used: Leaves

Remedial Uses: Astringent, uterine tonic, stimulant, parturient, vulnerary

History & Lore: Having the taste of black tea, red raspberry leaf is often used as a base in many herbal tea blends. It has been used by midwives for many generations, both during and after the birthing process, as a uterine tonic. It tones the uterus and strengthens the pelvic floor.

    Harvest the young leaves before the berries begin to show. Pick in late morning once the dew has evaporated.

Reishi
Ganoderma lucidum

Parts Used: Fruiting body

Remedial Uses: Anti-inflammatory, adaptogen, tonic, shen tonic

History & Lore: Reishi was once considered to be the "mushroom of immortality" and was consumed by ancient Chinese emperors to promote a long life, happiness, and well-rounded wisdom. Also called "the Great Protector" and "the Spirit Mushroom," reishi can be recognized by its glossy, reddish-brown skin. It is usually found growing on oaks, beeches, elms, and hardwood stumps.

Ganoderma tsugae is the North American variety of reishi, which can be found growing on hemlock trees in colder climates. Its properties are the same as *Ganoderma lucidum*.

Infuse reishi in cold water under the full moon for an extra-potent spirit-nourishing medicine.

Rose
Rosa spp.

Parts Used: Flowers

Remedial Uses: Aromatic, emmenagogue, uterine tonic, nervine, antispasmodic, aphrodisiac

History & Lore: Symbolizes love, romance, and devotion.

Considered to be the flower of Aphrodite, the goddess of love, in Greek mythology. Early Christians thought of it as the Virgin Mary's flower.

Rose has been valued throughout history for its use in perfumes. The scent is considered an aphrodisiac and antidepressant.

It is said that Cleopatra filled her living quarters with roses so that Marc Anthony would always be reminded of her whenever he came across a rose.

There are many varieties of rose. Always be mindful of harvesting from yards or using store-bought roses, as they are often sprayed with pesticides.

Self-Care

While sipping on a sweet and healing cordial can indeed be an act of self-care, there are many other ways to treat yourself with some love. Self-care is a sacred act practiced in many different ways across the world. Your practice may look drastically different from someone else's, but trust that you know what's best for yourself. No matter how you practice, it's important to take time for some self-love whenever you can. Wake up twenty minutes earlier than usual, brew coffee, grab a book or put on your favorite podcast, and take in the day as it is in that moment. Take a short walk and pay attention to the flowers and plants around you, or spend some time to write in a journal. Sit by a fire while slowly sipping your favorite cordial or tea, and be mindful of the rhythm of your breath and the air around you. Find what grounds and balances you, even if just for a few moments each day.

The following recipes, practices, and tools are meant to get you started and accompany you during your self-care routine.

Adaptogenic Sugar Rim

◇ 1/2 cup raw sugar or coconut sugar
◇ 1/4 cup dried rose petals
◇ 1 tablespoon maca powder

Place all the ingredients in a blender or food processor and blend into a fine powder.

To rim a glass: Pour the powdered mixture on a plate and wet the rim of a chosen glass with water or a wedge of fruit (limes and lemons work very well). Turn the glass upside down and dip into the sugar, making sure the mixture is evenly distributed around the rim. Add ice to the glass and pour your cordial or cocktail.

To Bathe in a Cup of Tea

What's better or more calming than a bath? A soak in a restorative tea.

I like to think of a bathtub as one giant teacup; it's the perfect vessel for herbal soaks and healing salty water. The following recipe should give you an idea of how to make an herbal salt soak. Gather whatever herbs or flowers bring you peace, and add those to the mix. If you don't have a bathtub, add this to an herbal foot soak.

◇ 1 cup Epsom salts
◇ 1/4 cup fresh or dried rose petals
◇ 1/4 cup fresh or dried St. John's wort
◇ 1 tablespoon fresh or dried sage
◇ 1 tablespoon fresh or dried chamomile
◇ 1 cup honey (optional)

Place the Epsom salts, rose petals, St. John's wort, sage, and chamomile in a large jar or bowl and mix well. Fill a tub with hot water and swirl in the herbal mixture. Add the honey, if desired, for increased healing. When draining the tub, use a mesh shower drain to catch the debris.

Golden Milk

A sweetly comforting drink. Ideal for chilly mornings or windy nights.

◊ **2 cups** milk of your choice
◊ 6 slices peeled ginger
◊ 1 cinnamon stick
◊ 1 teaspoon ground turmeric
◊ Pinch black pepper
◊ 1/2 teaspoon powdered ashwagandha root
◊ Honey or maple syrup, to taste
   (optional)

In a medium saucepan, bring to a light boil the milk, ginger, cinnamon stick, turmeric, pepper, and ashwagandha. Reduce the heat and simmer for about 10 minutes, stirring every 2 minutes. Remove from the heat, strain the mixture into a medium bowl, and return the liquid to the pan. Add honey to sweeten and whisk until the milk is slightly foamy. Serve hot or chilled.

Lavender & Chamomile Ice Cubes

These calming cubes make an excellent addition to any cordial, cocktail, or mocktail.

◊ 1 tablespoon lavender
◊ 1 tablespoon chamomile
◊ 1 tablespoon elderflowers
◊ 3/4 cup honey

In a medium saucepan, bring to a boil 2½ cups water, then add the lavender, chamomile, and elderflowers. Steep for 10 to 15 minutes.

Strain the mixture into a medium bowl and stir in the honey while the herbal water is still warm. Once the honey has dissolved, let the liquid cool, then ladle into ice cube trays and freeze.

Optional: Don't strain and leave the flowers in for an eye-catching addition to your final drink.

A Note on Wildcrafting

Wildcrafting is the act of venturing out into the wild with the intention of gathering wild herbs, fungi, and plants for medicinal purposes or food. Wildcrafting has been practiced throughout history and can be considered a sacred or even necessary act. It's always best to go about it with a basis of respect for the plants and the wild creatures that depend on them. If we overharvest from the wild, we run the risk of harming the natural process of growth and disrupting the rebirth and germination of a plant.

Here are a few basic rules for wildcrafting:

1. Never harvest more than you need. Most of the time, you do not need as much as you think you do.

2. Leave no trace. Be mindful of what you take into the wild with you and don't leave anything behind.

3. Only harvest what you know and even then, make sure you are 100 percent positive about your identification.

There are a lot of look-alikes out there that could be potentially deadly. Take an experienced friend or family member along or find a local wildcrafting/foraging workshop for extra support.

4. Get a good guidebook and ALWAYS take it with you.

5. Be respectful and mindful of the land that you are harvesting from. Be aware of the native and endangered plants in the area so you are careful not to disturb the natural habitat.

6. Keep in mind that you are a guest in the wild. There are creatures there that are much more familiar with the forest. Be smart.

7. Be mindful of where you are harvesting. Avoid gathering plants near busy roads and areas that have been sprayed with pesticides. Plants will absorb toxic waste and heavy metals from their environment.

Wildcrafting is a beautiful and meditative adventure. Enjoy it and take your time getting to know each forest, ocean, or desert and all the plants that grow there.

Bear in mind that it's not necessary to wildcraft everything. There are some quality bulk herb companies that I trust, and I've listed them in the back of this book. Or, if you are so inclined and have the space, you can grow your own herbs and mushrooms at home!

Flower Essences

While it may be obvious that plants have known chemical and nutritional value, they are also said to possess vibrational qualities. These vibrations are highly beneficial for emotional health and well-being. As a plant grows, energy is directed to different parts of its structure. Once a plant is in full bloom, most of its energy resides in the flower or fruit, making it the most potent part of the plant. This energy can be collected and utilized by infusing flowers into water in the sun or under the moon for a full day or night.

You can make your own essences or find them at most natural food stores. Bach Flower Remedies, Flower Essence Services, and Sister Spinster are a few of my favorite companies for purchasing flower essences.

Add a drop or two to completed cordials, cocktails, or bathwater.

Agrimony: Aids in working through emotional pain toward inner peace

Bach's Rescue Remedy: Functions as an excellent anxiety soother

Blackberry Lily: Releases trauma and fear from sexual history and past relationships

Holly: Helps deal with and minimize jealousy

Mimulus: Reduces anxiety and helps face fears

Poison Oak Flower: Enhances emotional intimacy and vulnerability

Self-Heal: Inspires healthful lifestyle choices

Yarrow: Offers protection; helps maintain healthful boundaries

Stones

While the general skepticism and attitude toward crystals is not lost on me, I must admit that I have a small collection, which I use daily. Most of the tincture blends I create for my online shop are infused with different stones in addition to herbs, just to give them an extra energetic kick. There is something magical about the elements of earth forming into something so beautiful and otherworldly, and for me, it's hard to fully deny the power crystals can have over our emotional well-being. So call crystal infusions alchemy, new age, witchcraft, or silly; I personally like to think of it as another way to serve your cordials "on the rocks."

To infuse: Drop the clean crystal of your choice into the jar along with your alcohol and botanical ingredients. Infuse and strain out the stones once the cordial has completed macerating.

Amethyst: Healing for grief and emotional pain

Citrine: Stone of success

Moonstone: Enhances feminine energy

Onyx: Increases emotional strength during times of stress or grief

Rose Quartz: Heart healing

Tigereye: Stone of protection and becoming grounded

Turquoise: Balance and wisdom

Recharge and cleanse crystals under a full or new moon.

Herbal Actions: A Glossary of Terms

Use the following terms to better understand and familiarize yourself with the function of each plant described in the *Materia Medica* chapter of this book.

Abortifacient: Substance that induces abortion

Adaptogen: Plant that helps your body adapt to stress and build immunity and that tends to work better when used frequently over time

Analgesic: Substance used to reduce pain

Anodyne: Herb that soothes physical pain

Antifungal: Plant used to prevent or treat fungal infections

Anti-inflammatory: Herb used to reduce inflammation

Antispasmodic: Herb that relieves muscle spasms

Antiviral: Substance used to prevent and ward off viruses

Aphrodisiac: Food, drink, or herb that arouses and stimulates sexual desire

Aromatic: Plant containing volatile oils that release scents that stimulate, soothe, or please the spirit and mind

Astringent: Substance that dries, puckers, and draws, either topically or internally, which helps create a barrier for healing

Bitter: Herb that increases bile flow in the intestine, thereby aiding the process of digestion

Carminative: Warming herb that promotes healthful digestion and eases bloating, constipation, and gas

Demulcent: Herb that produces a slimy substance that protects mucus membranes, soothes irritation of the digestive tract, and decreases inflammation

Diaphoretic: Herb that induces sweating

Diuretic: Herb that stimulates the elimination of fluid from the body

Emmenagogue: Herb that stimulates and increases menstrual flow

Expectorant: Herb that helps break up and expel mucus in the lungs

Nervine: Herb that is soothing to the mind and body

Nutrient: Herb that provides essential nourishment

Shen tonic: Herb that is nourishing to the spirit and emotional heart

Tonic: Substance that strengthens and rejuvenates the body over time; best used daily

Vulnerary: Plant used to aid the healing process of a topical wound

Resources & Plant People

Places to Buy Bulk Herbs

Frontier Co-Op//frontiercoop.com

Mountain Rose Herbs//mountainroseherbs.com

North Spore Mushrooms//at-home mushroom kits//northspore
.com

Starwest Botanicals//starwest-botanicals.com

Plant People

Other fine herbalists to know and love:

Rosemary Gladstar

Juliette de Bairacli Levy

Matthew Wood

Stephen Harrod Buhner

Susun Weed

David Hoffman

James Green

Deb Soule of Avena Botanicals

Dori Midnight of Dori Midnight Healing Arts

Summer Ashley & Sarah Kate of the Great Kosmic Kitchen

Siena Perez del Campo and Gabriel Vicente of Moon Minded Medicine

Milla Prince of The Woman Who Married a Bear

Liz Migliorelli of Sister Spinster

Maribeth Helen Keane

Brittany Ducham of Spellbound Herbals

Chanelle Bergeron of Moon by Moon Apothecary

Healing Books
(Healthy Meals to Pair with Your Cordials)

One Part Plant by Jessica Murnane

My New Roots by Sarah Britton

Nourishing Traditions by Sally Fallon

The Herbal Kitchen by Kami McBride

Acknowledgments

This book was a product of disbelief,
gratitude, and lots of giggling.
And the plants, of course.

Emma Brodie, my editor. I fully believe that you are some sort of witchy angel. I am in awe of your presence in my life and so grateful for the incredible belief you have in me. Leah Carlson-Stanisic for getting my "vision." I swear you have some sort of psychic insight into my creative mind. The rest of my HarperCollins team: Liate Stehlik, Lynn Grady, Cassie Jones, Susan Kosko, Rachel Meyers, Katherine Turro, and Bianca Torres. Thank you all so much for believing in this project and helping it to become a reality.

My mother, for believing in me regardless of how many times I told you not to. My father, for dragging me from store to store just to look at kitchen supplies. Who knew that all those hours of me sulking and complaining would lead to my own recipe book. Maria, for kicking my ass since day one on the playground/under the sink. You've supported me through the bad and a whole lotta good. Here's looking at a full lifetime with you by my side. Jill, for always knowing that I would write a book. And Sophie, for being my favorite little sister. Zoe and Andrew, for letting me spend hours sitting on your couch where I wrote a good portion of these recipes while you fed me rosé and other fineries. Zoe, you are my Piscean queen, and I'm grateful for your laughter. Marley Kehoe, for being my fake-ish agent and everything else, or whatever. The sweet, sweet community of supportive folk on Instagram and beyond. I honestly wouldn't be creating these zines, potions, and blog posts if it weren't for all of you. Thank you for the years of kind words and encouragement.

My entire family in Sweden, especially Anna, Hedda, Hilda, Lars, and Aunt Ewa. Britty Adelhardt, for being the first to read it. Catie Carl, for helping me with Photoshop. Chanelle Bergeron of Moon by Moon Apothecary, for all the support and calling it *Drunk in Love*. Sarah Morrison, formerly of Sparklehaus, thank you for naming Cinnapomme. Zwick, for the years of support and lessons. My incredibly supportive friends. I wish I could name all of you here on this page, but it would take another book for that. I am so blessed to have you all in my life. My island family, for shaping me into who I am now and providing me with some truly bizarre stories. Julia Bruner, my spirit sister. Molly Mugford, for always making me laugh. Andrea Bachman, for being my fancy hand model.

My Roots Sisters of Emerald Valley: The spirit and wisdom of you all is clearly formed in these pages; you are forever a part of my heart. All my teachers at the California School of Herbal Studies. Summer and Sarah of The Great Kosmic Kitchen, for being a huge support system and inspiration for me from the very start. Milla Prince, for being the loveliest recipe tester and contributor. Karen and Georgia of the *My Favorite Murder* podcast, for being the vocal backdrop to most of these pages. Also, the cast of *Jersey Shore* for being the background noise when I freaked myself out after listening to too much true crime in a camper in the woods of Maine.

Insty Print in Kalispell, Montana, for being so patient and printing out oh so many copies of my zines. And the badass women at the Kalispell post office. Aunt Karin and the Gibson guys, the Mizners, Maribeth Helen, Danny Fouts, Daytrip Society, Frinklepod Farm, Martha Lefebvre, Maggie Ruth, Erica Fayrie, Ian Ballard, the Sillén family, Gerry Holmes, Ben Walden, Connor Coughlin, the *Hauswitch* coven, Scott and Jana, Max Robinson, Jen Marlow, Laurie Irons, and Kris Mitzman.

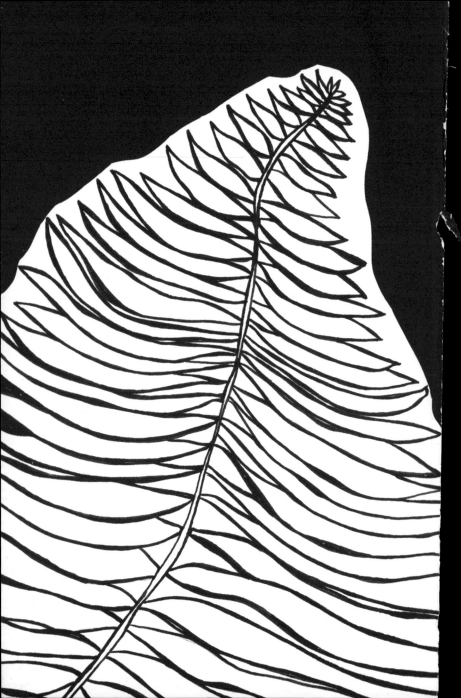